Katharine & Maurice George

MACKEREL THE TRAVELLING CAT
~ IN THE LAKE DISTRICT

with numerous illustrations
by
Jennifer M Toombs

and foreword by Chris Beetles

Green Dog Press

First published 2003
Published by Green Dog Press, 1 Church End, Swerford, Oxford, OX7 4AX, UK

Text ©2003 by Katharine K George and Maurice W George
Illustrations ©1999, 2003 by Jennifer M Toombs

ISBN 0 9538143 2 7 hardback
ISBN 0 9538143 3 5 paperback

British Library Cataloguing-in-Publication Data
A CIP catalogue record for this book is available from the British Library

OTHER TITLES IN THE SERIES

MACKEREL THE TRAVELLING CAT

~ BY THE SEA

IN PREPARATION:

MACKEREL THE TRAVELLING CAT

~ AT HOME AND AWAY

Printed in the U.K. by Classic Cheney Press, Banbury

By the time Mackerel had commenced his travels in Suffolk, described in *By the Sea*, he had become an accomplished fell-walker. He had already been taken twice to the Lake District in Cumbria in the north-west of England, and this book tells of the many times he spent there among the hills, during his adventures away from his Oxfordshire home.

Mackerel was a spirited companion in all weathers, placed his four feet firmly on all kinds of ground and encountered people and other animals in places as few cats have done. He was equally happy whether out on the fells or resting at the end of the day by the hotel fireside.

The Lake District will be familiar to many readers and those who have not yet been there might be tempted to venture among the fells. If there is an intrepid cat willing to go too, why not take him along …?

ACKNOWLEDGEMENTS

We are grateful to Norman Scarfe who kindly went through the draft, having already put us right where we had strayed in *By the Sea*. John Murray, whom you will meet from time to time in the book and who has climbed and lived in the Lake District for many years, also critically examined the text.

Peter and Sue Coward, managers of the Swan Hotel Grasmere 1973-1997, helped us to recall many happy memories, and provided the story of the 'volunteered guest'. John and Doreen Melling, who run the Glenridding Hotel on Ullswater, and all our other friends who knew Mackerel including those mentioned in the book, encouraged us and checked various facts and recollections, some going back nearly 20 years.

The authors are also thankful for the efforts of the National Trust and others which, over more than a hundred years, have magnificently sustained much of the character of the English Lake District.

In the Armitt Library and Museum in Ambleside, there is a rich legacy of paintings, drawings, prints and books all about the Lake District; some of those we have referred to are mentioned in the book.

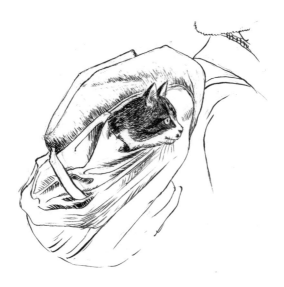

CONTENTS

FOREWORD 1

1. "WHY NOT TAKE HIM WITH US ...?" ... 3

2. OFF TO THE HILLS 7

3. HIS FIRST SUMMIT 11

4. MYSTERY 15

5. GRASMERE VALE 21

6. CAT BELLS 33

7. GHOST STORY 43

8. UNLIKELY ENCOUNTER 49

9. CHRISTMAS AT GRASMERE 55

FOREWORD

I've always felt that cats should get out more. They are happy to share the domesticity of the human condition and lazy comforts of the hearth all too easily. Ask any cat whether they fancy going down the supermarket or a quick trip to Benidorm and they will scratch, yawn and go back to sleep. However Mackerel is no ordinary cat. Not for him the easy-going limbo of the holiday cattery, instead he prefers the intrepid delights of Grisedale Pike, Helm Crag and the Old Man of Coniston. But mark this is no anthropomorphic tale – Louis Wain meets Monsieur Hulot's holiday.

Mackerel is always catlike, curious and involved but still a bit detached. Jennifer Toombs adds graphic delight to these travellers' tales with fine line and subtly hatched drawings complementing and even enhancing the fascinating narrative; each exquisite vignette adding naturalistic detail to this cheerful prose.

Forty years ago I fell in love with the Lakes on my days off from being a waiter at the Grand Hotel at Grange-over-Sands; long hot days 'o'er hill and dale' echoing Wordsworth, 'a mountain ascending, a vision of trees'. The enticing charm of this traveloguette has stimulated me to return. I have bought my Kendal Mint Cake, dubbined my boots and .....all I need now is a cat.

Chris Beetles is an art dealer in St James's London specialising in watercolours and illustrations. His annual exhibition Louis Wain and the Summer Cat Show *every August is the biggest event worldwide for original cat art collectors.*

Kirkstone Pass and Brothers Water

1. "WHY NOT TAKE HIM WITH US ...?"

Mackerel was born in the spring of 1983, in Oxfordshire near the middle of England. From a small kitten, he readily accepted being on a lead when taken for walks and he proved to be an excellent car traveller. When he was about five months old, the thought struck us: why not take him with us in February when we go for a short holiday to the Lake District in the north-west of England?   The Lakeland hills and mountains are tramped over by flocks of sheep, also countless human feet often accompanied by dogs, but at the time we had not heard of any cats going along too. No matter, we might find out if he liked it better than being left behind and perhaps gain some summits with four feline feet added to the party. So we began to think about what we needed to do to prepare Mackerel for such expeditions.

We remembered friends of ours who took their cat Doushka with them on their annual camping holidays. They took a very relaxed view of life and one dark night they backed the car up a track and managed to pitch their tent on some reasonably flat ground, only to find the next morning that they were in the middle of someone's front garden. When they knocked on the door to apologise, they were invited in for breakfast! Meanwhile Doushka had wandered off – but this was normal, he was no doubt supplementing his camp food with more natural fare, but he always returned when the time came to strike camp and

move on. We felt this to be altogether too risky – we had visions of Mackerel fleeing from unknown people or dogs, or disappearing down holes, even mine-shafts, of which there are many in the Lake District. Therefore, when away from home, Mackerel was always kept on his harness and lead.

Long after we had made our decision to take Mackerel to the hills we discovered an account of another mountaineering cat; A H Griffin in his book *In Mountain Lakeland* tells of the exploits of a Siamese cat called Rikki who freely climbed several tops with his mountaineering master including Helvellyn, over 3,000 feet high. But Rikki lived in the Lake District whereas Mackerel was only an occasional visitor and had no permanent home to return to after a day out on the hills.

Mackerel, unlike many dogs, was never prepared to remain for too long on all four feet without either demanding a rest, or wanting to indulge in his own investigations. When out for leisurely walks with us near home, such pauses or explorations were unimportant and in town he was carried, when necessary, in a small shopping basket. But in the hills frequent static contemplation of his surroundings was not practical, especially when with a party of friends, or when adverse weather threatened and time was running out for getting off the high ground before mists descended or night-fall arrived. To avoid this difficulty, Mackerel was given a rucksack into which he could creep and which was carried as a back-pack in the normal way, still leaving him able to look out, or tuck down out of sight, as he wished. This was tried on a few local walks, and Mackerel had no objection to this novel way of getting about. He was in good company, for Rikki once had a ride in his master's rucksack when he was unable to make headway in deep slushy snow. Eventually, after a few trips away, when Mackerel wanted a change from walking, he often rode outside on a shoulder, or on top of Maurice's rucksack which contained our needs for the day.

We decided that Mackerel should always have his daily meal in the car, and that he should sleep there as well if we had to stay in places where 'pets are not allowed'. These ideas were now tried out, to make sure that Mackerel would find them acceptable.

At home early one Friday evening, the car was parked outside the garage, the back seat laid flat, his supper and drink dishes put on the floor near the front passenger's seat, and Mackerel was introduced to his holiday headquarters. He stayed until the following Sunday morning, with a few walks on his lead and a brief trip to a nearby village on the Saturday. While he clearly did not understand the point of all this, he obligingly cooperated and enjoyed the fuss and attention. The arrangements were further successfully tested with an overnight stay with some old friends who lived about 50 miles away in Surrey.

February soon arrived and off we went for six day's holiday in the Lake District and Mackerel's first adventure far from home.

2. OFF TO THE HILLS

The distinctive part of the north-west of England that we call the Lake District is about 250 miles from Mackerel's home in Oxfordshire. It is roughly circular and only about twenty miles across but the scenery within it varies from serene lake shore and rounded hills to wild and craggy mountain tops, some over 3,000 feet high. This beautiful landscape has attracted poets, artists and increasing numbers of tourists.

Driving across country south of Birmingham, was to Mackerel no different from the many local rides on which he had already been taken, but joining the M5 motorway was a new experience. However, he was not seriously troubled, and especially after being told soothingly that the lorries were no danger to him, he began to get used to their passing roar. North of Birmingham we turned off the motorway and found a quiet lane for a brief stop for all of us to stretch our legs and take some quick refreshment. Mackerel was given a drink from a small bottle of water kept handy in the passenger's door compartment. We then kept going steadily, Mackerel dozing on the passenger's lap and occasionally showing interest when something new attracted his attention.

After leaving the motorway at Penrith, at the north-east corner of the Lake District, we were soon driving along the western side of the angled reaches of Ullswater. For most of its nine miles length the road winds by the lake shore until towards the head of the lake the hills begin to dominate the scene; Place Fell fills the view across the lake, the fells guarding either side of the Kirkstone Pass lie ahead, and the hills of the Helvellyn range loom large to the right. We spent the next two nights near the head of the lake in the village of Glenridding, at the hotel of that name. Mackerel was to stay there and explore the surrounding country almost every February for the next twelve years.

Clarke's *Survey* of 1792 marks a house which has been developed into the hotel we see today. However, despite modern additions one can still imagine horses and carriages in the roadway. The car-park can be reached directly from the road through a covered way through the middle of the building or from a short lane which leads down to the edge of the lake and to Glenridding Pier.

Just beyond the head of the lake and a mile from Glenridding is the village of Patterdale where the old, stone-built parish hall has been converted into a climbers' hut which is shared by the Tuesday Climbing Club (T.C.C.) and the Association of British Members of the Swiss Alpine Club. Every February the T.C.C. holds its annual dinner at the Glenridding Hotel, which the authors of this narrative, having been associated with the club since it was founded in 1957, always made sure to attend. As it was not practical for Mackerel to be in the hut we stayed in the hotel. When we told the reception that our cat was in the car, and asked if we could bring him in, we were told that, well, er, *dogs* were allowed in – other than in the restaurant of course – on payment of a small charge.

The proprietors John and Doreen Melling decided that Mackerel was an *honorary dog* and he was consequently admitted. It turned out that this was a great favour, as the Mellings had a resident dog, a smooth, grey-haired whippet. Mackerel did not abuse his privilege, being content with hunching his back if Shandy came too close.

Rising from the open reception area and bar-lounge is a fine carpeted staircase, a continuous flight of eighteen steps to the first floor, but for weary souls, exhausted after a hard day climbing, there is a small lift. This contrivance astonished the cat, particularly as there are four alternative floors to be confronted with: the two bedroom floors, the reception floor and, below that, a cold, narrow passage with a low ceiling, leading directly outside into the covered way. After one or two annual visits he became used to it and was no longer startled by the sudden opening of the door, with no-one touching a handle! Even with a year's break between, when coming out of the lift, he always got ready at the correct side of the door. Our room overlooked the head of the lake and the lane leading down to the pier, and Mackerel's mobile headquarters could be seen safe in the car-park below.

The next day Mackerel was introduced to the novelty of exploring the paths and lake shore nearby. The following morning we packed our bags, said goodbye to our climbing friends and paid a visit to Haweswater, the easternmost of the lakes. After a short walk there, we drove round the Helvellyn range to the village of Grasmere.

There we introduced Mackerel to Peter and Sue Coward who ran the Swan Hotel, where we were to spend the remaining four days. But the next morning all exciting plans were dashed – both his mentors woke up feeling unwell and were still no better after breakfast. Both being too ill to go out in the car, the doctor was called in.

"Acute bronchitis, stay indoors!" he ordered.

After four days he signed his patients off fit to go home and back to work the next day. The first evening arriving home after a long day, Mackerel was there at the drive gate to greet us, full of purr, which showed very clearly he had enjoyed his adventurous holiday and wouldn't mind going on a few more.

Grasmere Vale and Dunmail Raise

3. HIS FIRST SUMMIT

To make up for those four missed days, the end of April saw the three of us back again at the Swan in Grasmere, now with fine weather and with the high fells topped with the remains of winter snow gleaming in the sunshine. Mackerel realised "Oh – we've been here before!" Then a short walk up nearby Greenhead Gill caused him to anticipate that perhaps it was going to be "like that other holiday ..."

The next day started sunny but also being fairly cool it was ideal for something energetic. Half a mile away, going up towards Dunmail Raise, the Keswick road passes over the beck from Tongue Gill which runs steeply down the fellside to join with Raise Beck and form the river Rothay. From the bridge an old, rough path leads over the fells and then down to Patterdale and Glenridding. The top of the pass is Grisedale Hause, where, off to the right is the way up to the summit of Fairfield, 2,864 feet high, the object of the day's expedition.

For setting out from the Swan, Mackerel was put in his rucksack but as soon as we left the road and joined the path, his rucksack was placed on the ground, out he stepped and his walk began. With a little encouragement he soon set off, sometimes ahead, but usually between us with master leading. At first, Tongue Gill beck is in a deep wooded ravine to one side and hills rise ahead. Where the beck divides and an old miner's path leads off into Little Tongue Gill, Mackerel's world expanded.

A wooden bridge over the main beck had to be crossed, much bigger and higher than the plank over a little stream near his home. Having safely negotiated that, he peered through a fence round a small reservoir, glanced at the remains of mine buildings by the beck and then pressed on up the main valley with many more pauses to look at the scene ahead and the way back. Cats are always inquisitive, looking around all the time, forever cautious and liking to be sure of their surroundings.

The view back down the valley is at first dominated by the bulk of Helm Crag blocking the distant scenery to the south and west, but higher up it opens out until the crag appears a modest part of the foreground with the ridges of Langdale and the Coniston Fells stretching out behind. Mackerel was attracted to a large detached overhanging boulder lying a few yards to the right of the path; he walked all round it and enjoyed the novelty of the cover it provided.

We stopped for a rest and some refreshment at the confluence of two of the headwaters of Tongue Gill beck. We were now near the head of the valley with only a short steep climb ahead to Grisedale Hause. Nearby a waterfall cascaded down in a curtain of rivulets and we were surrounded by the sound of water splashing its way over rocks and through pools to join the stream below. But, what was delightful for us to hear and see, was for Mackerel suddenly overwhelming. Perhaps he felt like Alice when she ate a piece from the right-hand-side of the

mushroom and had shrunk to a fraction of her
normal size. His environment suddenly seemed to
be towering all round him and had become too
much for his young brain to take in. Half shutting
his eyes he laid his ears back and said "Meow!"
He crept into the shelter of his rucksack where he
stayed for the climb to Grisedale Hause with
Grisedale Tarn spreading below it but soon
afterwards he began to peer out occasionally to
look at his surroundings. At the top of the steep
stony path which leads to the summit of Fairfield,
Mackerel's courage returned and he emerged into
a beautiful day with patches of snow glistening in
the sunlight. He walked along the edge of a snow
patch and joined in a game of snowballs.

Arriving at last at the summit cairn, we could
see the Pennine hills to the east and the highest
Lakeland peaks of the Scafell group to the west.
Looking northwards and to the right of the bulk of
Helvellyn, the long ridge of St Sunday Crag; to
the south, Coniston Water and Windermere
gleamed in the distance. After enjoying the view
and a bit more rest, we set off on the long sloping
ridge which goes almost due south down to Rydal.
Mackerel seemed to sense that we were now on the
way back to base and trotted along at a brisk pace.
On leaving Great Rigg we turned to pass over the
rocky shoulder of Stone Arthur making for
Greenhead Gill, familiar from the previous day's
walk, and back to Grasmere.

That day, Mackerel's fell-walking career was
launched; he led some of the way up and most of
the way down and was not too tired but more than

ready for his supper. He had walked nearly six of the seven mile circuit over which he had climbed some 1400 feet and descended more than that. At that time he had only a short lead attached to his harness. It is difficult to keep an even distance behind a cat who might suddenly stop for reasons apparent to him but not to his minder, so for the next climbing holiday an extending lead was purchased, which made cat management much simpler and gave Mackerel far more freedom and enjoyment.

4. MYSTERY

On our regular February visits to Glenridding for the T.C.C. club meet, we always hoped for some snow to provide extra interest for both climbing and the scenery. Once, when the weather did oblige, we were tramping in thick snow with two friends on the slopes of Red Screes, above the head of the Kirkstone Pass, when we found that someone had made a shelter out of blocks of snow, like a small igloo. Inside it was remarkably comfortable and warm with room enough for one person and a cat. Mackerel and his guide would have happily settled down there for the rest of the day, but were overruled by a majority of three to two.

Another time when it was freezing hard several groups of club members had set off to climb in various directions from the valley of the Glenridding Beck. High winds forced changes of plan and we all converged near the old lead mines, where the buildings had been converted into holiday accommodation and a youth hostel. After a sheltered spot was found on the hillside for a break, because the weather was not getting better, we all decided to return to Glenridding. We went by the path along the side of the valley rather than down the old mine road; the going was straightforward until we came to a large sheet of ice which could be avoided only with a very awkward scramble. Mackerel put everyone to shame by using his built-in crampons to tread daintily across the ice and then watching us

Treecreeper

humans struggling our way round to him. Cats have distinct advantages on rock and ice.

The lane to the pier at Glenridding is flanked on one side by a field which stretches between the lake shore and the Patterdale road, and on the other by a verge and the Glenridding Beck. The verge broadens towards the lake with a mixture of grass, and stony ground, trees with low branches and knobbly trunks and a few holes and surely lots of interest for a cat? For some reason Mackerel never liked being taken there for his morning and evening walks and no amount of coaxing persuaded him that there was nothing to worry about. The field however was perfectly acceptable and he soon became used to taking his mentor across the lane, through a small gate and over to what became his favourite spot under the trees, alongside the Patterdale road. Was the presence of St Patrick's Well across the road a calming influence?

We thought Mackerel was just being fussy but when we happened to mention this to our friend and T.C.C. member, John Murray, he was astonished. To our surprise his own dog Jen, an intelligent Border collie, also hated that area and whenever John took her for a walk down the lane she had the same strong reluctance. We could not think of any obvious reason for this mysterious behaviour, but whatever the cause, the two animals independently detected something which made each of them feel uncomfortable.

During the winter a year or so later, John and Jen made national news. Jen was with her master

near the top of Helvellyn, the second highest mountain in the district, when she fell through a snow cornice. There are always cornices on Helvellyn after even a small amount of snow, due to the escarpment along the summit ridge. John spent many hours over several days looking for Jen below the crag. At last, when he was almost at the point of being forced to give up, two climbers spotted her, perched on a small ledge where she had landed and from which she could not escape. With the intelligence of her breed she did not risk a further fall and survived by licking the snow. From their vantage point the climbers were able to direct John to the spot and his dog was safely rescued. Apart from being cold and hungry Jen was otherwise unharmed and was soon back to full health and vigour. The story appeared in newspapers with a photograph of them both.

Mackerel visited most of the interesting places near Glenridding and one of our favourite summits overlooking Ullswater is Glenridding Dodd which commands views over the upper reaches of the lake, over 800 feet below. The path from the village is now quite distinct but only a few years ago we had to make our own way up the steep slopes. Mackerel was often a help in such conditions; by pulling on his lead he provided a significant upward force for his companion. Cats are quite strong and it was an unexpected bonus to be able to use his strength to good purpose.

Another place he went to is the great waterfall of Aira Force, the biggest waterfall he

would ever see but by then no longer a spectacle to overawe him.

Aira Force and the adjacent Gowbarrow Fell was the third of the many places in the Lake District brought under the protection of the National Trust. The falls can be crossed at two stone bridges: one at the top of the falls, and another at the bottom. The water leaps out from under the upper bridge, hurls itself down, and when the beck is full after rain, fills the ravine with spray as it bounces off the rocks into a pool, before escaping under the lower bridge and rushing down the valley towards Ullswater. When standing near the lower bridge on a sunny day, a rainbow can be seen in the spray. The lower bridge, built in 1932 to replace a wooden one, is dedicated to the diplomat Sir Cecil Spring Rice who wrote the words of the hymn *I vow to thee my country*, often sung to a rousing tune by Gustav Holst.

In the peaceful wooded valley above the waterfall there are further smaller cascades and the beck tumbles over and round rocks in between which are a series of clear pools with overhanging branches, an ideal spot for a dipper – a little grey bird with a white breast. We saw one perched on one of the rocks using it as a look-out, from which it flew into the water but then continued to fly, completely submerged, for up to perhaps half a minute, catching its food. It returned to its rock, unafraid of our presence and in spite of Mackerel's pricked ears and look of amazement.

Other places in the area that we explored included walks around the head of the lake and along the shore of Ullswater below Place Fell, and up to the small, secluded Hayeswater reservoir. Because of the shortness of the winter days, expeditions to the higher fells at Mackerel's pace would have taken too long; these were saved for later in the year when we stayed at Grasmere or in Borrowdale.

Immediately opposite the Glenridding Hotel there is a path going alongside Glenridding Beck from which we climbed up to a tiny stretch of water called Lanty Tarn, one of several places in the Lake District reputed to be associated with Lanty, a miner and smuggler. We went on into the beautiful valley of Grisedale, between Helvellyn and St Sunday Crag. This is particularly attractive in the low winter-morning sunshine when the water gleams as it tumbles down over the rocks. We have also walked from near Hartsop to beside Brothers Water; some say that this is so called because two brothers, while skating there, fell through the ice and were drowned. From there we sometimes continued on into Dovedale where once, after saying goodbye to friends who had to journey back home, we climbed up to where the snow was still lying and we had the valley to ourselves.

Ullswater

5. GRASMERE VALE

Grasmere is a village of character with a network of footpaths within its bounds and many lovely walks beyond. The poet William Wordsworth lived in Grasmere and then in nearby Rydal from the age of nearly thirty until his death in 1850 when he was eighty. He extolled the beauty of Grasmere vale in prose and poetry and indeed the valley still has its own unique charm. The village has grown since those days, boats can be hired by the Langdale road, there are many more visitors and there are probably a few more trees, yet it is still easy to recognise the scene described by William Hutchinson in 1773. He wrote in his *An Excursion to the Lakes* that he and his companion were

> ...charmed with the view of GRASMERE, a retirement surrounded by hills on every hand; the vale contains a four miles circumference of meadow and pasture ground; – near the middle of this valley is a fine lake, beautified with an island. – From a mount (a little distance from the church) we viewed the whole circle, delighted with the situation; – the fields were full of freshness and verdure, the scene was ornamented with a few humble cottages dispersed on the borders of the lake, amongst which, the sacred fane [church] stood solemnly superior; – the hills were here and there graced with a few trees, and animated by white flocks of sheep. – It seemed to be the vale of peace.

There are ways through the encircling fells between Nab Scar and Loughrigg Fell to the south and over the crest of Dunmail Raise to the north.

The intriguing outline of Helm Crag dominates the northern view, and, depending on where you are standing, its summit rocks are seen either as a lion and a lamb or an old woman playing the organ.

Mackerel explored all the village paths and crossed the river Rothay at various bridges many times. One pathway used to go through the school playground, where Mackerel would be wary of the children. Now a footbridge commemorating the Millennium provides a better route out of the village alongside part of the river and across the fields to the main road and the Swan.

The Swan hotel, originally an ancient wayside inn on the road from Ambleside to Keswick at the foot of the pass of Dunmail Raise, lies on the edge of Grasmere village with open fells rising behind it. To increase the accommodation over the years, a succession of small extensions has been added on at the back. The entrance, which faces onto the road, goes straight into the sitting area, with its welcoming log fire and low ceiling supported by exposed oak beams. The staircase, which is in front of you across the room as you go in, leads, with two turns, to the original few bedrooms above, and to a door opening into a corridor with a creaky floor. More doors and several further turns, steps and stairs lead to the more recent parts of the building. The newest rooms, being by now some way up the hill, have views up the valley to Helm Crag and Dunmail Raise. We used to stay in one of these and Mackerel took only a few visits to learn which way the doors opened and which was our room. Soon he would purposefully lead the way. A small parking area at the same level as the most recent extension enabled us to put the car in a relatively secluded spot not far from our room. Over the following twelve years the Swan came to be almost like a second home to Mackerel.

The Swan is commemorated by Wordsworth in his poem *The Waggoner*. Benjamin is driving his waggon through from Ambleside on his way to tackle the steep gradient of Dunmail Raise, a mile or so ahead. Thirsty work and a good drink to help him on his way is a temptation. He bravely passes by one alehouse, the DOVE & OLIVE-BOUGH (which Wordsworth hints was to become his own home – hence *Dove Cottage*) but a mile further on he reaches the SWAN "Inviting him with cheerful lure ... Of open house and ready fare." The poem goes on to describe the inn-sign:

> Who does not know the famous SWAN?
> Object uncouth! And yet our boast
> For it was painted by the Host;
> His own conceit the figure planned
> 'Twas coloured all by his own hand;
> And that frail Child of thirsty clay,
> Of whom I sing this rustic lay
> Could tell with self-dissatisfaction
> Quaint stories of the bird's attraction!

As if to re-assure the contemporary reader, or perhaps mollify mine host of his time, Wordsworth provides the following footnote:

> This rude piece of self-taught art (such is the progress of refinement) has been supplanted by a professional production.

Although in Wordsworth's time the Swan was a simple hostelry, when we first stayed there it had been a comfortable hotel for more than a

hundred years but still retained its links with the past. A chair in the sitting-room is reputed to have come from Wordsworth's last home at Rydal Mount. Those poetically inclined can sit in the chair and hope for the muse to favour the sitter with inspiration.

Mackerel was with us at all times in the hotel except for meals so, after being taken for his early morning walk, he stayed in the car while we had our breakfast. When the time arrived for everyone to have their evening meal, one of us always took Mackerel to the car for his supper and a peaceful hour or two for him to relax. Later Maurice would collect him to join us while coffee was taken by the fire and we either read or chatted with other guests.

Thus the routine became established. Mackerel often led the way into the room looking to see where Katharine would be sitting. He always sat quietly, or gave himself a wash, unabashed by the expressions of wonderment from any of the guests who noticed him. Sometimes people spotted him only when the time came to retire, seeing him go up the stairs on his way to the long corridors to our room.

Because of its closeness to the back of the Swan, many walks were taken up into Greenhead Gill. The beck running past the Swan flows out of the gill and several small caves can be found in the hillside alongside it. These are the remains of the 16th century Grasmere lead mine and although they interested the cat we did not explore any of them – entering old mine workings is strictly only

Greenhead Gill

for experts with the appropriate equipment. Three paths start on the other side of a gate at the end of a short lane that climbs steeply uphill alongside the beck. One crosses over the beck on a plank bridge where Mackerel usually paused to look over the edge at the water rushing by, a dozen feet below. Going up the gill, the beck can be crossed back and forth at several places and it was here that, for the first time, Mackerel picked his way carefully across a beck. A few yards above the bridge, a path to the right leads abruptly up the fellside to Alcock Tarn. The mixture of rock and grass makes this a grand walk in miniature with superb views across to the high central fells and, two miles away, the foaming waters of the magnificent Easdale cascade. There is also a fine birds-eye view of Grasmere village and the lake with its wooded island. The descent to White Moss Common then past Dove Cottage makes a fine circular walk at all times of the year. Even in November the combination of low sunshine and mist can be magical.

The Easdale cascade can also be seen as a white wraith against the not so distant hillside from the little wooded, rocky hill in Grasmere village, called Butherlyp How with its fine mixture of trees. One of the most popular excursions from Grasmere since people began walking in the fells for pleasure is to pass close by the cascade and go on up to visit Easdale Tarn. The walk from the village green begins gently uphill and, passing by the few outlying houses and farms, leads to a path and a bridge over the confluence of two streams.

Further on to the left, Blind Tarn Gill is at most times a friendly enough place, but is very different in the depths of a hard winter. In Wordsworth's time, there was a cottage in which a man, his wife and their eight children lived a hard-working and frugal life. In 1808 both parents died in the snow when trying to struggle their way back from a sale over in the neighbouring valley of Langdale. Their children were left destitute and Wordsworth's sister Dorothy related in a letter to a friend how she and her brother helped to organise their support to prevent the youngsters "... falling into the wrong hands".

Soon the path becomes more rocky, and narrows as it enters Sourmilk Gill. Here Mackerel would wait while parties of faster walkers strode by. At last the cascade we could see from the village appears on the right. Above it the way becomes less steep and, after a curve to the left, leads to a valley with rocky faces ahead and on either side, in the centre of which is Easdale tarn, a third of a mile across. Nearby, overlooking the tarn, is a large rocky slab beside which is a heap of stones. These are all that is left of what was once a refreshment hut, where the thirst of Victorian walkers was slaked and which was still a recognisable ruin in the 1950's. After reaching here, we often crossed the beck where it issues from the tarn, dropped down into Far Easdale and joined the path which comes over from Stonethwaite in Borrowdale. We would then follow this back down towards Grasmere, past a variety of tall, stately trees planted over a century

Allan Bank

ago as if in a park. Now a metalled road, the route crosses a flat meadow with sheep grazing, and joins the road leading back into the village. Mackerel did this walk several times and the varied nature of the landscape always provided plenty of interest.

On the west side of the village, forming a ridge linking Loughrigg Fell with the head of Easdale is Silver Howe with two main paths crossing it leading into Langdale. One of them leaves the Langdale road near the boat landings and offers walkers many fine views to linger over. The other path goes from the centre of the village past Allan Bank where the Wordsworth family once lived and were plagued by smoking chimneys and damp cellars. Further up the Langdale road a path leaves the steep hill called Red Bank and slants gently down across the side of Loughrigg Fell with views over the length of Grasmere, its village and Dunmail Raise in the distance. This is Loughrigg Terrace, a popular walk with its pleasant broad path that Mackerel liked well enough, although he was always wary of other visitors. The way continues on past Rydal Water near to which is the great cave of Loughrigg. This large cavity in the fell-side was formed from slate quarrying.

On our many journeys from Grasmere over Dunmail Raise to the north-western fells we passed alongside Thirlmere, especially liking the quiet road on the western side of the lake, from where Mackerel once explored among the trees and becks flanking the lake on a walk up to

Harrop Tarn and back. The road past Thirlmere was the route taken by Wordsworth and Coleridge, when they walked the thirteen miles to visit their friend and fellow-poet Robert Southey at his home in Keswick. The rough track of those days eventually became the only main road through the middle of the Lake District but relative peace has returned to the valleys now that heavy commercial traffic has been diverted away to the outskirts of the area.

Thirlmere in Wordsworth's time was a shallow, picturesque lake that, at its narrowest point towards the northern end near Armboth, could be crossed by a rustic bridge. The lake was dammed, the foundation stone laid in 1890, to transform it into one of the largest in Cumbria, to provide water for the city of Manchester nearly a hundred miles away. The water still flows to Manchester and a fountain opposite the Town Hall, fed from the supply, was opened with great ceremony in 1894. By tunnelling through or contouring round hills and crossing over gills and valleys, the engineers achieved a tiny but steady fall of about seven feet every four miles – a gradient of about one in three thousand – so that the water flows all that way by gravity alone. Above the Swan the enclosed aqueduct can be seen where it crosses Greenhead Gill in a fine stone arch. The aqueduct is mostly underground but the route is kept under surveillance and until a few years ago this was done by a man walking the route from end to end, taking several weeks. We

Fly-Agaric

met him once at Greenhead Gill, carrying keys to all the gates along the way.

Hidden from the village, the other side of Helm Crag is the less frequented Greenburn valley. Mackerel became familiar with this quiet area, which although close to Grasmere is yet somewhat 'off the beaten track'. At its foot, rising to over a thousand feet on either side, are Helm Crag and Steel Fell. There is no lake or tarn but because there is no big fell at its head the valley is never gloomy even when the sky is overcast. While Steel Fell does not have the dramatic outline of Helm Crag, its secret is its northern prospect over Thirlmere to the imposing peak of Skiddaw and the north, which springs into view as a reward to the climber on reaching the summit cairn. There is also a route which goes up the valley alongside the beck with its cascades, shared with the local sheep, that leads up to a mossy cove from where the surrounding ridge can be easily reached.

The round of the valley's enclosing fells from Steel Fell to Helm Crag is a pleasant grassy walk with further stunning views from the summit of Helm Crag over Grasmere village and lake, and the expanse of Lake Windermere beyond. The second time Mackerel went up Steel Fell we made the round with our friend John Murray and his dog Jen. Jen was quite young then, and she spent most of her time chasing birds; when she became tired of this and drew too near to Mackerel he peremptorily indicated that she should keep her distance. While he went steadily ahead keeping to the main route Jen bounded around in wide circles

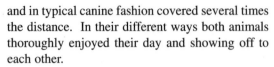

and in typical canine fashion covered several times the distance. In their different ways both animals thoroughly enjoyed their day and showing off to each other.

Our route to the Greenburn valley from the Swan was either up the main road to cross the beck which runs down from Tongue Gill or, more interestingly, along a footpath through a couple of fields and crossing the beck lower down, using stepping stones. Mackerel tolerated water rather better than it is generally supposed that cats do. He was not frightened of crossing the mountain becks and seldom even got his feet wet. Here however, things did not go as planned.

As we approached the side of the beck, Katharine and I saw a couple ahead decide against the stepping stones and turn away towards the main road. Although running with a fair flow of water the top of the stones were well clear so we decided to cross. I went first allowing Mackerel's lead to reel out behind me. Reaching the far bank without mishap I then called him to follow. Mackerel had reached the penultimate stone when he missed his footing, slipped and fell right into the water. With a rapid scramble he landed at my feet. Katharine then made to follow but almost at once she lost both her nerve and her footing, filling her boots with water. Faced with wet cat my side of the rushing stream and wet wife the other, there was no alternative but to return. Putting Mackerel, who had already started to lick himself dry, under my arm, I went back across the stones, thankfully arriving safely on the other side.

A towel was always kept in Mackerel's rucksack for rubbing him down if it rained and he got too wet. It was put to good use and soon both cat and Katharine were well dried off. After using the alternative route by the road we all reached Greenburn to enjoy the rest of the walk. Mackerel was very sure-footed and the adventure remained a singular event leaving him unperturbed by the watery encounter.

Thirlmere

6. CAT BELLS

Mackerel was an experienced shopper, so a visit to Keswick and wandering around the market square with its Moot Hall built in 1813, was taken in his stride. A short drive away is the ancient stone circle of Castlerigg, which may be up to 5000 years old. The setting is dramatic with a panorama of fells to the south and, to the north, Saddleback, still often called by its older name Blencathra. Although this is a very open scene with little cover Mackerel did not mind, neither did he react in any way to the stones, regarding them as he might any other boulder encountered on his walks, even though stone circles are places where sensitive people can detect unusual natural forces.

A couple of miles to the south with the road from Thirlmere to Keswick on one side and the vale of St John's on the other is a rocky fell called High Rigg. High up among trees against the northern flank of the fell, and reached by a steep and winding road, is the little church of St John's. It is a short way from the church to the high point of the fell with views north to Skiddaw and Saddleback, and south to Thirlmere flanked by the Helvellyn range. Mackerel enjoyed this walk, and the summit cairn, which he visited several times.

Derwent Water, with its two wooded islands, was sometimes called 'Keswick Lake', the town being at its north-east corner. The road from Keswick to Borrowdale alongside the eastern shore of the lake has several stopping places with

views at lake level. The quieter road along the western side is much higher up and has a spectacular view over the lake to Walla Crag. It was on this road that Mackerel observed some bad manners. When we stopped the car to enjoy the view over Derwent Water, some sheep that had been standing nearby gathered round the car clearly demanding to be fed with something different from grass. When we declined to give them anything they threatened to attack our car with horn and hoof, forcing us to drive away before they could damage the paintwork. This road was the starting point for our next adventure.

Cat Bells? No, not for attaching to Mackerel's harness so that if we could not see him in a thick Cumbrian mist we could at least hear him, but a popular peak on the west side of Derwent Water with one of the best views of Skiddaw. With a name like that, it was agreed that we had to introduce Mackerel to it. However, not all writers agree on whether the name has anything to do with wild cats and Mackerel gave no impression of being aware of his distant ancestors being present, in neither corporeal nor ghostly form. The three of us followed the well-trodden path up the northern slope of the fell, now and then remembering to turn to see the view of Derwent Water which steadily unfolds, until on reaching the top, the whole lake is displayed over a thousand feet below, with Keswick and Skiddaw at its lower end, and the village of Grange at its head. Mackerel led most of the way up to the summit, clambering eagerly over grass and rocks alike.

THE NATIONAL TRUST

CAT-BELLS RIDGE

Although it was a fine day there was a wind from the north which became stronger as we ascended. This did not bother Mackerel at first but by the time the top was reached it became almost impossible for him to look round – the wind kept blowing his ears inside-out! He crept into the shelter of his rucksack and was carried until we left the ridge for less exposed paths when he resumed his walking and completed the circuit back to the car.

Little Town is a farming hamlet in the Newlands valley nestling against the west flank of Cat Bells. 'Little-town' was the home of Lucie who found the tiny door in the side of Cat Bells in Beatrix Potter's *Tale of Mrs Tiggy-winkle*. Newlands was indeed 'new land' when in the 12th century a shallow lake called Husaker was drained to provide agricultural land. A track leading into the valley originally gave access to a series of mine workings from which various minerals were extracted for several centuries, and which have left their mark on the landscape. The first miners came from Germany in the 16th century and extracted lead from the Goldscope mine on the far side of the valley. R G Collingwood in *Elizabethan Keswick* tells us that the name is a corruption of the German *Gottes Gab* (God's gift') and nothing to do with the small amount of gold found there. The main track runs close to several later copper mine workings on the side of Maiden Moor, the higher southern neighbour to Cat Bells. Each old mine provided an exciting hole to be explored and we were thankful that the more precipitous ones

were adequately fenced to prevent us from falling in – Mackerel tugging hard might have caused a *cat*astrophe. With his wanting to explore every hole he came across, progress was slow and before we reached the head of the valley the weather intervened. We retreated by the way we had come, pursued by lowering clouds and drenching rain over the last mile of the walk. This time, instead of getting into his rucksack, Mackerel kept dry by tucking himself in under the front of Katharine's zipped up anorak.

On the opposite side of Derwent Water, two miles from Keswick, Walla Crag soars above the woods. The ascent from the Great Wood car-park is a route of contrasts. The start is on a broad, steadily rising track through woodland up which Mackerel trotted with nothing of particular interest to distract him. On leaving the wood there is a grassy area with hedges and a stile. Further along at the top of the cliff there is a different world again, with natural rockeries to scramble among and heathery patches to burrow through, making it fascinating for the cat. There are stupendous views across Derwent Water to Cat Bells and the rounded knob of Causey Pike, and further away to its right, dominating the skyline, is the elegant shape of Grisedale Pike. Almost beneath our feet, were the tops of trees growing against the steep cliff face, which gave Mackerel a kind of view which he had never had before, looking directly *down* into the branches where *birds* live. He wisely made no attempt to explore over the edge into this sylvan world but followed the descent down a steep path at the edge of the wood alongside the aptly named Cat Gill.

One afternoon we set off from Grange at the head of Derwent Water, with our friend George Hall, a member of the Fell & Rock Climbing Club for over fifty years and first president of the Tuesday Climbing Club, to ascend King's How, the summit of nearby Grange Fell, on the east side of Borrowdale. Climbing up the path through the woods to King's How there are glimpses of Derwent Water and the fells beyond. At the top the full extent of the lake over 1,000 feet below and the view all around can be appreciated. This relatively unfrequented spot is an outstanding viewpoint and Mackerel again enjoyed the heathery landscape and lack of competing humans. King's How forms one of the steep sides of the narrow valley through which the River Derwent emerges from Borrowdale. The crags near here provide sport for rock climbers, while below them is the Bowder Stone, which has long been an attraction for tourists.

Bowder, according to the Oxford English Dictionary is an old north country word meaning *boulder* and that is what it is – a mighty boulder. It weighs around 2,000 tons but some old guide books quote various weights, one asserts it to be 1,771 tons 13 pounds! It rests, seemingly precariously, about 100 feet above the road and the River Derwent. The stone was probably left in its present position following the retreat of the glaciers at the end of the last ice age. It is like a giant cube and appears to be balanced along one

edge embedded in the ground. Some timid souls are nervous of going underneath it, fearing that any minute it will topple over. Others, more daring, provided they have long arms and don't mind lying on their stomachs, can shake hands with each other through a small hole underneath. The walk to the stone from the National Trust car park is through woodland, along an ancient rocky path which used to be the only way into the heart of the Borrowdale valley beyond. Nowadays, because of the trees, the stone is invisible until one is almost upon it, unlike the open landscape shown in early drawings or photographs.

On reaching the stone, Mackerel was confronted by the long wooden staircase which leans against its side. After a brief inspection, he ran up the steps to the top of the stone from where there are views up and down the valley and across to Castle Crag. When seen from the north Castle Crag appears to block completely the way through what is called the 'Jaws of Borrowdale', but from the Bowder Stone the road can just be detected through the trees below, winding alongside the river Derwent. It was driven through rocks around the 1830's, by-passing the old track past the stone. After investigating the grooves now polished by the seats of several generations of explorers, Mackerel was persuaded to leave his airy perch and descend, which he did with characteristic caution.

Castle Crag is almost surrounded by the remains of an old slate quarry and some stretches of the path to the top are over waste material from

the quarrying. As one walks over the loose slates they often make a ringing sound and by collecting slates of differing lengths and thickness a musical scale can be created. The Victorians excelled at this sort of thing and in the Keswick museum there are fine examples of whole instruments of stone. As a schoolboy Maurice watched *The Bluebells of Scotland* being softly drummed out by the elderly curator with his knuckles on a large 'stone organ' which made an unforgettable, haunting sound. The summit of Castle Crag is a tiny world of grass and rocks and birch trees making it an exciting place for cats and other explorers with chinks and corners and good shelter from the wind for picnics. The view down the valley to the north is of Derwent Water and Skiddaw. Southwards, the broad hidden valley of Borrowdale can be seen, surrounded by hills and crags.

We stayed several times in Borrowdale at Hazel Bank, on the edge of the village of Rosthwaite, traditionally associated with the Herries novels by Hugh Walpole. The path from Rosthwaite over to Watendlath in the neighbouring valley passes close by, and Mackerel went on several walks along it including one where, after leaving Watendlath, a path goes southwards through a mixture of bog and heather and leads to the peaceful waters of Dock Tarn. We descended by Willygrass Gill into the Stonethwaite valley and back to Rosthwaite.

Rigghead quarry lies across the valley from Hazel Bank, about a thousand feet above the village. The approach is a delightful walk through

Sundew

a farmyard, across the river Derwent and then up a steep and stony gill. A few rusting remnants of the equipment once used to transport materials from the quarry could still be seen when we were there, but once into the quarry the main interest is the caves left by the miners. Mackerel was fascinated by them and again had to be restrained from climbing into potentially dangerous places. Above the quarry and a further climb past Dale Head tarn led on to the summit of Dale Head from where we saw the almost aerial view into Newlands valley.

One morning we set off with George Hall in the same direction from Hazel Bank. When we arrived at the bridge over the Derwent and where the path to Dale Head begins, Katharine and Mackerel continued on their own along the footpath by the river and through the woods to Grange. There, they sat outside a little café, one having a cup of coffee while the other settled himself down and, mostly unobserved, quietly watched folk come and go. Meanwhile the other two walked over High Spy, and then came along the ridge to drop down into Grange and rejoin Mackerel and his minder for all to spend the rest of the day going over King's How.

On an earlier occasion we had all climbed High Spy together and Mackerel stood on the summit. After leaving to descend towards Grange, we had to follow an indistinct path leading off the ridge. Finding this point was always a matter of debate which Mackerel left to the humans and simply enjoyed the dramatic descent into the valley.

Skiddaw and Derwentwater from King's How

At the head of Borrowdale branching to the left is the great valley of Langstrath, from where the Stake Pass leads into Langdale. Ahead is the way to Seathwaite, the wettest inhabited place in England, the Styhead Pass and the highest fells. To the right is the way to the Honister Pass. Also ahead and often rising into the mists, are the high hills of Glaramara with Scafell Pike and its neighbours beyond.

Mackerel ascended Glaramara twice. The first time we were with friends including George, John and Jen and we walked from Rosthwaite. The second time George was again with us and we started from Seathwaite where we left the car. Going over Grains Gill at Stockley Bridge took us up to Styhead and the highest pass in the Lake District at Esk Hause – 2,490 ft. From there over Allen Crags to Glaramara one walks into the view, which from the summit of Glaramara is perhaps the finest panorama in the district with Borrowdale and Derwent Water in the middle ground and distant Skiddaw as the backcloth. On the descent we missed the way to Seathwaite so we continued the walk down Thorneythwaite Fell to the road at Strands Bridge. There, Katharine rested with Mackerel, both sitting on the bridge parapet while the other two walked back to fetch the car.

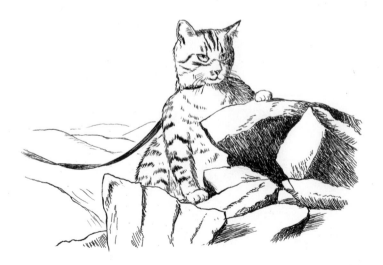

Path down from Fairfield

7. GHOST STORY

Ambleside, an old market town where the River Rothay runs into the head of Lake Windermere, was once the site of a Roman fort. It lies between Loughrigg Fell and Wansfell with the Fairfield group of fells to the north. Behind Loughrigg Fell is the pretty Loughrigg Tarn surrounded by woods and gently sloping grassland, with animals grazing down to the water's edge. We walked round the tarn with Mackerel and had a picnic on a bank where there were patches of delicate white violets.

A big attraction in Ambleside for Mackerel's two mentors, but not one he was allowed to enter, is the Armitt Library and Museum. This insufficiently known Cumbrian treasure-house was founded in 1912 by the will of Mary Armitt. She was one of an influential circle of friends which included Hardwick Rawnsley – writer and a founder of the National Trust, Beatrix Potter, John Ruskin, and many others all of whom knew and loved the Lake District and its people. They corresponded with those of like mind and accumulated books, manuscripts, objects and pictures of all kinds relating to Lakeland interests. Valuable, and often unique gifts, and purchases when funds permit, continue to be added to this day. Beatrix Potter bequeathed her exquisite watercolours of fungi, lichens and mosses to the library, which were the product of some of the meticulous and original scientific work she did before Peter Rabbit and his friends appeared.

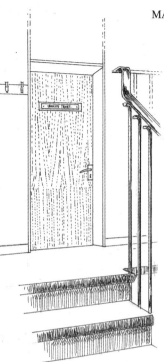

Evidence of the Roman occupation of the area is displayed, including an inscribed tomb stone and in a showcase there is a model of the Roman fort. All this is now beautifully shown in a new building opposite the main car-park in Rydal Road. In Mackerel's day, everything was squeezed into one room above the public library and the great bulk of the collection was stored out of sight. He would be left snoozing in the car in the small car-park across the road while we spent a happy hour or two reading scarce books and pamphlets, or, wearing the white cotton gloves provided, looking at folios of superb drawings and engravings of Lakeland scenery. As always we were made welcome and helped by one or two of the team of volunteers without whom the Armitt would remain permanently closed. Clare Brockbank, for many years one of the trustees and a volunteer, is appreciative of cats, so Mackerel had the privilege of being introduced to her. As the Armitt does not specifically allow cats to enter, greetings were exchanged on the doorstep at the top of the stairs.

Along the road from Ambleside to Coniston is a turning off to the hamlets of High and Low Tilberthwaite. A track from Low Tilberthwaite leads to an area where copper has been mined from the time of Elizabeth I until the workings were finally closed in the 1970's. With many holes and caves to explore, Mackerel looked as far as he could into every one he came across. The track climbs high along one side of a steep sided gorge, with a worked out slate quarry on the opposite side, after which it broadens out and the valley floor shows the signs of many mine workings. While most of the big holes are fenced one cannot be too careful in avoiding shafts and pits that are partly hidden by overhanging branches and other vegetation. Mackerel had to be kept on a tight lead to make sure he was not too adventurous.

When travelling in the car from the Coniston area to Ambleside, for a change we decided to use the chain ferry which crosses Lake Windermere. The ferry worked by dragging itself along the chains which stretch across the lake between the ferry landings. After the ferry moved off we got out of the car with Mackerel to see the view, but he looked cross, disliking the clanking and rumbling noises – not the sort of sound to be expected from a boat.

One day we set out to climb the Old Man of Coniston, that is the *mountain* of that name, the highest of the fells overlooking Coniston Water. Rising out of Coniston village is a steep road which is the start of an ancient track-way known as the Walna Scar Road. It is metalled for about the first mile, then becomes a broad mountain track which goes across to Dunnerdale, the valley of the river Duddon, the beauty of which inspired Wordsworth to write a series of sonnets.

Soon after setting out we caught up with a *human* old man and, in the tradition of walkers and country people, we passed the time of day. He was going in our direction so we continued together and chatted. He told us that during the year he was walking up to the summit of the

Old Man a hundred times for charity and had achieved some publicity for it. He also told us that he was a retired Merseyside police inspector and that he had taken part in the early episodes of *Z Cars*, a popular television programme. Further up the hill and well beyond the village we came to a level stretch of road with hedges on either side. He related how early one morning at this very spot, he was sure he saw a ghost. He told the story of a young girl who had been murdered here and sometimes appears to travellers along this road. Early morning mist can take many forms and give rise to stories like this one, nevertheless, he impressed us with his account – but Mackerel gave no hint of sensing anything strange.

By now we were not sure of getting back in time for supper so we changed plans and decided to see Goats Water, a tarn hidden the other side of Old Man. We said "Cheerio" to our companion as he turned off to the right to make another ascent of the mountain. We continued along the Walna Scar Road with views of Coniston Water receding behind us. After about another mile we turned right, up a path alongside a stream, which led into a boulder-strewn valley, almost enclosing Goat's Water except where we clambered through by the stream, with Dow Crag and the Old Man towering 900 feet above us.

Mackerel was not over-awed and enjoyed exploring among the rocks. On our way back there were occasional patches where water was flowing across the track. Mackerel did not mind this and stepped happily through; at one moment

he seemed almost to walk on its surface as he delicately forded a sheet of shallow water lying across our path.

It was near here that Mackerel astounded two energetic young men who were rapidly descending the track. As they sped past, one of them remarked to the other,

"They say you see things after drinking *Smirnoff,* but after only one cup of coffee – well, this is ridiculous!"

Saying no more, they disappeared down the hill.

Buttermere

8.   UNLIKELY ENCOUNTER

"How many lakes are there in the Lake District?" you ask. "One hundred?" "No." You keep on saying no to your victim until they give up.

"One!" you say triumphantly, laughing at your victim's look of disbelief. "Bassenthwaite Lake – all the others are *waters, meres* or *tarns.*"

Indeed a count of all the stretches of water in the Lake District runs into hundreds but curiously, only the most northerly of the big lakes, Bassenthwaite, is usually called a lake. However, in early guide-books it too is referred to as Bassenthwaite Water, or Broadwater. Overlooking the far end of the lake, Sale Fell is a gentle hill on the extreme north-west edge of the Lake District, which Mackerel ascended one day, plodding about 600 feet uphill with his long lead stretched out. He was probably pleased to get out after a wet morning shopping in Cockermouth.

Between Keswick and the lake is a road, which branches off westward, through the village of Braithwaite and goes up nearly 800 feet to the Whinlatter Pass. In the 1920's, Arthur Hope, a far-sighted headmaster of the Roan School for Boys in Greenwich, London, bought an old mining hut and had it transported from the other side of Skiddaw to outside Braithwaite, near the bottom of the pass. With this hut, he established a permanent camp-site for the Roan School. After Arthur Hope died, the Braithwaite Camp, as it is familiarly called, was named the Hope Memorial Camp.

Except during the world war, it has been used ever since by Roans and by other schools. It was from here that Maurice first set foot on the Cumbrian hills, which he has visited regularly ever since. It was therefore natural that some of our walks were here in the north-western fells and that Mackerel was introduced to this varied, beautiful and sometimes challenging landscape. Near the top of the pass is the Whinlatter Forest Visitor Centre opened by Sir Chris Bonington, the distinguished mountaineer.

The Centre is the focus of public access to the Whinlatter Forest Park, and provides much information on the trees and wild life of the park. One of the displays is a larger than life model of a badger sett through which you can walk. This was irresistible to Mackerel who led us into its dark passage as if on one of his nightly prowls at home. Listening to the surprising sound of a badger crunching his supper and then being confronted with a badger three times life size, left the cat unfazed with his unerring dismissal of anything he recognised as not natural and therefore best left to humans.

Choosing a walk on the north side of the Centre we made our way up through the woods until the path became steep and muddy but the terrain improved and soon we reached a clearing and the rocky summit of Seat How covered with heather and bilberry. The views of the fells are dominated by Skiddaw and Saddleback across the plain between Derwent Water and Bassenthwaite Lake; nearer is Grisedale Pike, just across the valley. On our return, the muddy slope proved a trial for human feet so branches and tussocks had to be clutched to prevent a glissade but the cat's four feet with his claws gave him a perfectly controlled descent.

Mackerel climbed Grisedale Pike starting from a short way up the road from Braithwaite. A forest track took us out on to the open hillside, where, turning to look, we were greeted with a view of the whole Skiddaw range. We then ascended the airy ridge of Sleet How to the top of the pike. It is a rewarding summit with the cliff of Hobcarton Crag to one side, all the major Lakeland peaks visible to the south and distant views of the Scottish hills to the north. We went onwards round the head of the Coledale valley along the narrow edge to Sail and returned to Braithwaite through Barrow Door, a gap in the hills, which for young enthusiasts makes many a fine photograph from the Hope Memorial Camp. A tired trio arrived rather late that evening and very ready for supper, having completed one of the best circular walks in the district.

A few years later, we set off to ascend Grisedale Pike again. Because it was Maurice's first Lakeland summit it became a family tradition to attempt the climb every decade, near or on the anniversary day. This time we drove over the Whinlatter Pass to the foot of the great valley of Crummock Water and Buttermere. We stopped at Lanthwaite Green and walked up the broad rocky ravine of Gasgale Gill which ascends in a gentle curve to Coledale Hause. After reaching the hause

we climbed to the top of Sand Hill, about a mile from the pike and only little more than 100 feet below it. However, in between there is a dip of 250 feet; it being a lovely clear day, Katharine decided against going down to go back up again and preferred to sit comfortably in the sunshine with the cat and look at the view. Maurice set off while the other two watched his progress. Mackerel did not like this and wanted to follow but instead had to gaze, with a worried look, after his master's diminishing figure. The ceremonial visit to the summit was rewarded with distant views all round. Mackerel was greatly pleased when Maurice arrived back and all cheerfully went back down the gill and returned to Lanthwaite Green.

On another visit to the same valley, but starting from near Gatesgarth farm at the head of Buttermere, we followed the path which leads over a pass into the head of Ennerdale. This is Scarth Gap, and from here Mackerel scrambled up a steep, rocky slope to the left and onto the relatively level ground on top. The name of the fell is Haystacks, well called after its shape, and a significant place for all fell-walkers: here were scattered the ashes of that giant among the writers of Lake District guide books, Alfred Wainwright. Without his drawings and detailed descriptions, many paths in the area would be generally quite unknown. 'A.W.' regarded Haystacks as the best top of all for variety and enchantment with its mixture of rock, heather and tarns and excellent views in all directions. We descended at first towards Honister and then turned down the old quarry road, which made a good way down back to Gatesgarth.

We also walked one day from Buttermere village alongside Sail Beck which has steep banks filled with woodland, ferns and wild flowers. Emerging from there onto the fells we partly ascended Whiteless Pike. It was here, high up on the open fellside, that Mackerel first met a Herdwick sheep, and we don't know who was the more surprised.

9. CHRISTMAS AT GRASMERE

"We'll all have figgy pudding..." goes the carol but fortunately Mackerel didn't hear it and was not tempted to disturb his diet with unusual Christmas fare. Carols were sung just before dinner on Christmas Eve when he was already eating his own supper in the car. But he always joined in afterwards while all of us listened to the Kirkby Lonsdale handbell ringers or to local schoolchildren singing carols. That was the start of Christmas at the Swan as guests arrived to a friendly welcome from our hosts Peter and Sue Coward and made new acquaintances or renewed old ones. English weather being what it is, over seven years we had everything from snow, rain, wind, to clear blue skies and brilliant sunshine. Our experiences out and about were similarly varied. There was always an expedition on Boxing Day and a guided walk the day after that and Mackerel came on most of them.

Watching the weather on Christmas Eve the question was: shall Father Christmas come tomorrow morning on a sledge? He did on some occasions but not while we were there, so we only saw his surrogate sledge – a small pony-cart provided by Sue Coward and drawn by her little Shetland pony called Dougal. Father Christmas himself is a friend of the Cowards, blessed with a real and magnificent white beard and moustaches. He always arrived in his 'sledge' ringing a bell and carrying a sack of presents for all the guests. To

prepare for this Sue contrived every time to bring Dougal secretly from his field opposite the Swan, round to the back of the hotel and harness him to the pony cart. They were then decorated with garlands, not forgetting a pair of antlers for Dougal. After Father Christmas climbed aboard with his sack Sue then led them along a convenient loop road to emerge a hundred yards down the main road (no traffic on Christmas morning) from where they would triumphantly arrive in front of the Swan to loud cheers from the assembled guests.

During the lunchtime festivities, Mackerel rested quietly in the car and then sat by the fire as we digested our meal. The evening brought the chef's magnificent decorated buffet, complete with a life-size sculpture of a swan made of solid ice. More entertainment then followed for which Mackerel again joined us, although he did not personally develop skill at dominoes.

In the morning on our first Boxing Day, after a night of heavy rain we drove through floods and strong wind to Bowness on Windermere, where we boarded a hired motor cruiser for a trip on the lake. This was Mackerel's first proper voyage, his previous excursions on water – not counting the oddity of the chain ferry – having been in a canoe under June sunshine on a placid mere in Suffolk. Windermere was very rough with waves breaking over the bow of the boat and there was a great hubbub in the cabin. When this was combined with the noise of too many crackers being pulled at once, we retired to the deck where Mackerel

simply blinked and looked at the scenery shrouded in rain. He accepted it all as just another unusual event and cheerfully divided his time between the fun in the cabin and the stormy prospect from on deck.

The following year Boxing Day was a complete contrast; it was a beautiful day with the lake and surrounding hills looking as if they had been taken from Italy in the summer. A picnic lunch was provided in the cabin, with Christmas crackers after which most of the time was spent on deck enjoying the views of the Langdale Pikes and, at the head of the lake, the hills of the Fairfield horseshoe. After landing back at Bowness, we all went to the newly opened Beatrix Potter Experience, where the world of Peter Rabbit and his companions is shown in a winding corridor, lined with a succession of dioramas with life-size representations of the animals that appear in Beatrix Potter's stories for children. We asked, could we take Mackerel in? The question was greeted with much surprise but permission was readily granted when it was seen how well he behaved. He saw the stuffed animals and birds and dismissed them as fakes, although he did prick his ears at a handsome magpie.

Our first walk after Boxing Day was a circular one that took us into Langdale for a pub stop. We went over the snow covered shoulder of Silver Howe and down some steep and precipitous paths. The snow was several inches deep and Mackerel's pace would have been slow so he rode in his rucksack for the whole of the trip and

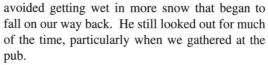

avoided getting wet in more snow that began to fall on our way back. He still looked out for much of the time, particularly when we gathered at the pub.

Another year, on a bright sunny morning enhanced with wreaths of mist, we all climbed Latrigg a mile north-east of Keswick. On the way we drove past Thirlmere, where the surrounding fells were perfectly reflected in the surface of the still water. We parked near the former Keswick railway station from where a winding lane joins a path up to Latrigg. It is a steady climb and Mackerel made good progress with everyone else. At the 1203 ft summit we were treated to a splendid view of Derwent Water softly lit, while beyond the lake we could see Borrowdale filled with bright morning mist with the higher fell tops appearing above it.

Sometimes we extended our holiday beyond the Swan's three-day Christmas break which gave us time to go into Grasmere and visit the bookshops – readers familiar with Mackerel's adventures in *By the Sea* will recall his liking for them. One is Sam Read's at the corner of the village green, which sells new books and maps. Once inside Mackerel would settle down, clearly at home with the scent and general atmosphere of books. Further through the village from the church and across the bridge over the river Rothay, was the Bridge Bookshop where John Taylor's second-hand books provided us with happy hours of browsing. Having been persuaded to leave the first shop Mackerel always eagerly entered the next one, to sit quietly by each book-case in turn as we investigated the contents for items of interest.

On our way to and from the Bridge Bookshop or from the garden centre across the road where the mixture of different plant scents gave Mackerel much to think about, we often passed through the churchyard or visited the church with its unusual roof construction. How this came about is explained in Mary Armitt's *The Church at Grasmere*. The village population increased with the expansion of the wool trade in the 14th century and the church was doubled in size by the addition of a broad, north aisle, with its own pitched roof. However, water and snow which collected between the new roof and the old, caused endless trouble until in 1562 the will of a parishioner gave money "... so that the roofe be taken down and made oop againe." The local builders boldly extended the old north wall upwards to support the ridge of a new pitched roof over the whole building, leaving much of the interior woodwork untouched. This gives the inside of the church an unusual appearance, but bright and lofty with the clear east window. The churchyard has the graves of Wordsworth and his family. Also to be seen is the grave of William Green, who died in 1823. He was an artist who produced several splendid series of engravings and etchings showing both the interest and beauty of the Lake District from grand scenery to village streets. He also wrote the first straightforward tourists' guide to the Lake District. The Armitt Library and Museum has early editions of his books, many of his original drawings and

paintings and copies of all his principal work, including his coloured aquatints.

On three of those Christmas breaks we fell victim to *influenza*. At first we conveniently took it in turns so that one of us was always available to take Mackerel for his walks morning and evening. But the third occasion we were both ill with high temperatures, so neither of us could go out. Being confined to our room by illness or inclement weather was never too hard to bear because we could all see the ever-changing views from our window. Indeed, the window ledge was a favourite perch for Mackerel and he often jumped on to it as soon as the door was closed and we released his lead. However, *both* of us being ill barred either of us from taking Mackerel out for his morning and evening walk, not even to the bottom of the garden underneath the bushes, especially as it was freezing outside with ice and snow. Looking at Mackerel as he stretched himself on his mat, the maxim came to mind: "... never under-estimate the intelligence of a cat." We telephoned Sue and told her of the predicament.

Sue, having now known Mackerel for many years, reassured us, confident that everything would be all right. And so it proved. The hotel staff began to vie with each other as to whose turn it was to be cat minder and as each walk-time came round, we began to wonder who next would arrive to collect him. On one occasion two young waitresses appeared at the door, anticipating their task with barely suppressed laughter. Mackerel rose to the occasion and his behaviour was exemplary, winning the heartfelt admiration of all his minders and our grateful thanks to all of them. He had a favourite fencing post by the hotel where he regularly sharpened his claws; every time he led the way to it then continued to a suitable spot to dig his 'garden'. One evening, with snow on the ground, Sue 'volunteered' one of the guests! Peter, hearing of this, mischievously photographed the guest being pulled across the back car-park making it appear that Mackerel was taking *him* for a walk on a lead.

With the festivities over, the time had come for Mackerel to shuffle off his harness and resume his mousing duties and guard-cat patrols. We returned to our home refreshed, to welcome in a new year and look forward to our next visit to the Lakes in February, meeting Jen and Shandy again and our other climbing and Glenridding friends.